538
C

Guy B. Teachey School Library
Asheboro, North Carolina 27203

MAGNETS

Ed Catherall

Silver Burdett Company

Fun with Science

Electric Power　Hearing　　　　　Clocks and Time
Solar Power　　Sight　　　　　　Levers and Ramps
Water Power　　Taste and Smell　Magnets
Wind Power　　 Touch　　　　　　Wheels

ECIA-86-87
First published in 1982 by Wayland Publishers Limited
49 Lansdowne Place, Hove, East Sussex BN3 1HF, England

© Copyright 1982 Wayland Publishers Limited
Published in the United States by
Silver Burdett Company, Morristown, N.J. 1982 Printing

ISBN 0-382-06652-9
Library of Congress Catalog Card No. 82-50138

Designed and illustrated by Chris Smithers
Typeset by Plus 5 Limited, London
Printed in Italy by G. Canale & C.S.p.A., Turin

Contents

Chapter 1 Magnet power
What will your magnet attract? 4
Which is the strongest part of your magnet? 5
Through what will your magnet act? 6
Will your magnet act through metal? 7
Is the magnetic force weakened by passing through things? 8
Measuring the strength of your magnet 9
Making a magnetic racetrack 10
Making magnetic word games 11

Chapter 2 Making magnets
Making a temporary magnet 12
Making a permanent magnet 13
Taking care of magnets 14
Making a magnetic compass 15
Making a floating compass 16
A magnetic compass and magnets 17
Magnetic attraction and repulsion 18
Comparing the strength of magnets 19
Patterns with magnets 20
Magnetic fields 21
Making pictures of magnetic fields 22
Three-dimensional magnetic fields 23

Chapter 3 Electromagnets
Magnet power from electricity 24
Making an electromagnet 25
Making stronger electromagnets 26
Making electricity from a magnet 27
Making a transformer 28
Using magnets 29

Chapter 4 The Earth as a magnet
Using a magnetic compass 30
The Earth's magnetic field 31
Making a model of the Earth 32

Chapter 1 Magnet power

What will your magnet attract?

Collect magnets of different kinds.
Sort your magnets according to their shape.
How many of your magnets have a keeper?
Remember to replace the keeper when you store your magnets.

Select a strong magnet. What will this magnet attract?
Make a list of all the things that your magnet will not attract.

Make a list of all the things that your magnet will attract.
Can you feel the magnetic force when your magnet attracts a large object?
Write down what material you think each object is made of.
What do you notice about the things that are attracted by a magnet?
Does your magnet attract everything made of metal?

Test coins to see if they are attracted by a magnet.
Pure nickel coins are attracted. Coins made of a copper-nickel alloy will not be attracted, as the alloy contains only a small amount of nickel.

Which is the strongest part of your magnet?

Which part of your magnet did you use to attract things?
What happens if you use the middle of your magnet?

How many tacks or small nails will your magnet pick up?
How many tacks or small nails can you hang end to end from one place on your magnet?

Measure the length of a bar magnet.
Use a pencil to mark regular distances along your magnet's length.
How many tacks can you hang from each pencil mark on your magnet?

Draw your magnet with tacks hanging from it. What do you notice about the number of tacks hanging from each point?
Is your drawing different from the picture on this page?

Repeat this experiment using other bar magnets. Which is the strongest magnet?

What happens if you try this experiment with a different shaped magnet?

Through what will your magnet act?

Place a tack on a wooden ruler.
Move your magnet underneath the ruler.
Does your magnet act through wood?
Can your magnet pull a tack up a sloping ruler?

Place a tack in an empty glass jar.
Can you lift the tack up the side of the jar using your magnet outside the jar?
Does your magnet act through glass?

Put a tack in a jar full of water.
Hold your magnet in the water.
Is the tack attracted through the water?
Does your magnet act through water?

Wrap your magnet in a piece of paper.
Does your wrapped magnet attract a tack?
Does your magnet act through paper?

Put your magnet into a plastic bag.
Does your magnet act through plastic?

Will your magnet act through wood, cotton, nylon or rubber?
Make a list of all the things through which your magnet will act. Remember to try different liquids.

Will your magnet act through metal?

Wrap your magnet in metal foil. Does your metal-wrapped magnet attract a tack?
Does your magnet act through metal foil?
Which metal is your foil made of?
Does your magnet attract this metal?
Tape your magnet to a wooden ruler so that the magnet sticks out beyond the end of the ruler.
Hold the ruler in a stack of books.
Tie a thread to a metal paperclip.
Make sure that your magnet attracts the paperclip.
Use a tack to fasten the other end of the thread to a block of wood.
See that the paperclip does not touch your magnet.
Can you get your magnet to pull the thread taut?

Put a coin between the paperclip and the magnet. What happens?
Does your magnet act through the coin?
Does your magnet attract the coin?

Cut the top from a metal can.
Hold the can lid with a pair of pliers.
Place the can lid between the magnet and the paperclip. What happens?
Does your magnet act through the can lid?
Does your magnet attract the can lid?

Is the magnetic force weakened by passing through things?

Use sticky tape to fix a tack to a length of thread.
Tape the other end of the thread to a wooden ruler.
Hold the ruler in a stack of books so that the tack hangs freely.
Slowly, move your magnet towards the tack.
Measure the distance at which the tack first begins to move towards your magnet.
Record this distance of attraction.
Try not to let the tack touch your magnet while you do this experiment.

Place a sheet of paper between your magnet and the tack.
At what distance will your magnet move the tack?
Record this distance.
Compare the two distances of attraction.
Is the magnetic force weakened by passing through paper?
Does it matter how many sheets of paper you use?
Is the magnetic force weakened by anything through which your magnet will act?
Try some metals. What happens?
What happens if you use a can lid?

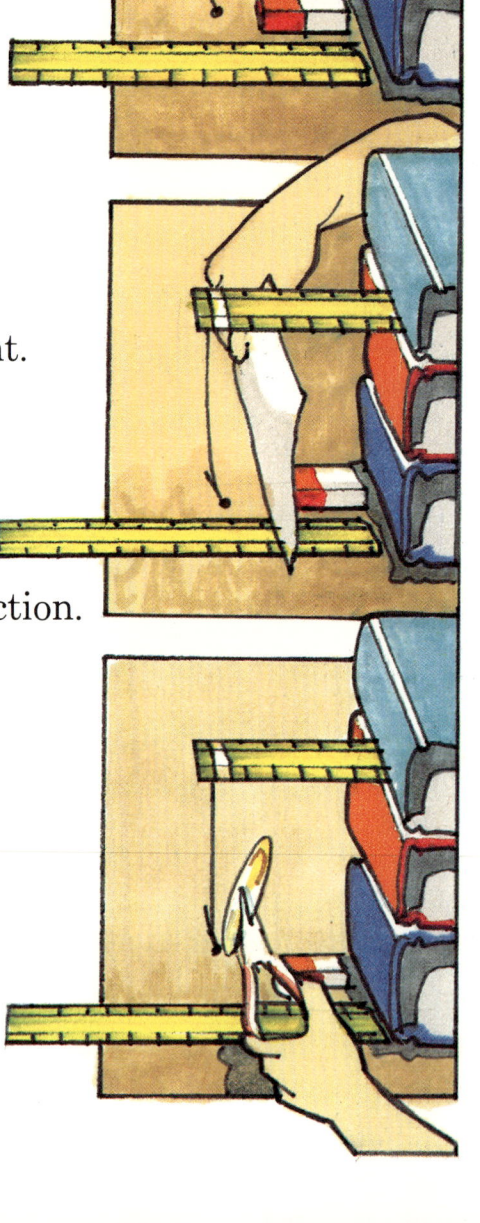

Measuring the strength of your magnet

Make a bridge by supporting a wooden ruler between two stacks of books. Stand a bar magnet on your wooden bridge.

Make a hook from a metal paperclip. Check that the paperclip is attracted to your magnet. Place the hook under your wooden ruler. Does the magnet hold the hook to the ruler? Measure the thickness of your ruler. This is the distance from your magnet to the hook. Hang paperclips on the hook, one at a time. How many paperclips can your magnet hold up?

Make a bridge using two wooden rulers. Does your magnet hold the hook through two wooden rulers? Measure the thickness of both rulers. This is the distance from your magnet to the hook. How many paperclips can your magnet hold up? Repeat the experiment with three rulers. Record your results.

Test the strength of your magnet through cardboard, stiff plastic lids, and glass microscope slides. Record your results.

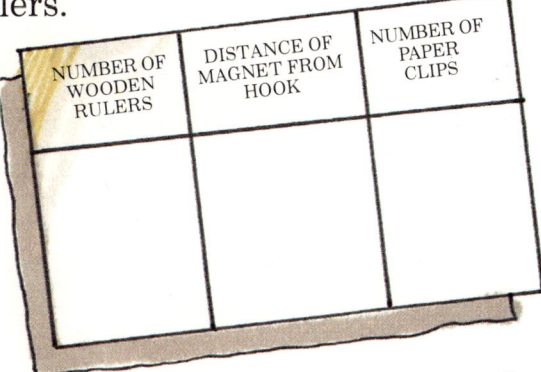

9

Making a magnetic racetrack

Find a steel ball bearing the size of a glass marble.
Put the ball bearing on top of a large sheet of strong cardboard.
Hold the cardboard above a table by using books at the corners.
Tape your magnet to a wooden ruler so that the magnet sticks out beyond the end of the ruler.
Move your magnet underneath the cardboard.
Does your magnet pull the ball bearing along through the cardboard?

Cut out a circle of metal foil.
Press the metal foil onto your ball bearing to make a tadpole shape.
Check that the ball turns freely within the tadpole shape.
This tadpole is your racing car.
Does your magnet pull your racing car along through the cardboard?

Mark out a racetrack on your cardboard.
Guide your car around the track using a magnet under the track.
What is your best time for one lap?
Can your friend beat your time?
Make two racing cars.
Race them around your track using a magnet for each car.

Making magnetic word games

Cut out some small squares of paper. Attach a paperclip to each square. Find a weak magnet. Will this magnet pick up a paperclip attached to a paper square? Use sticky tape to fix a length of thread to a magnet. Tie the other end of the thread to a stick.

Write a different letter of the alphabet on each square of paper. Make some extra squares with vowels on them.
Put the paper squares, each with its own paperclip, into a deep cardboard box.
Use your magnet to fish out the letters.
Make words with the letters you fish out.
When you have made a word, put the letters of that word back into the box.
Play this game with your friend. Decide on your own set of rules. How do you think this game should be scored?
Should all letters be worth the same number of points?
What other magnetic word games can you design?

Chapter 2 Making magnets

Making a temporary magnet

Find a large iron nail.
Does this nail attract a tack?

Does your magnet attract the iron nail?
Put the head of the nail against one end of a strong magnet.
Now will your nail attract a tack?
Can your nail pick up the tack?
Slowly remove your magnet from the head of the nail. What happens?

Put your magnet close to the head of the nail. Make sure that your magnet does not touch the nail.
Does your nail attract the tack?
Can your nail pick up the tack?
How close to the nail must you hold your magnet for the nail to lift the tack?
How far away from the nail can you hold your magnet and still attract the tack with the nail?

Leave the nail attached to your magnet for an hour.
Can your nail now act as a magnet on its own?
How long does your nail stay magnetized on its own?
What happens if you do this experiment using a wooden stick instead of an iron nail?
What happens if you use a brass nail?

Making a permanent magnet

Find a steel knitting needle. Does this knitting needle attract a tack?

Put the knitting needle on a table.
Hold it with your finger and stroke the needle thirty times with one end of your magnet. Make sure that you always use the same end of your magnet. Always stroke your needle in the same direction.
Can your needle pick up a tack? How many tacks can you hang from the end of your needle?

Stroke your needle another thirty times. Make sure that you use the same end of your magnet and stroke in the same direction as before.
Now how many tacks can you hang from the end of your needle?
Is the needle more magnetic?

Try to make a really strong magnet.
What is the greatest number of tacks that you can hang on the needle?

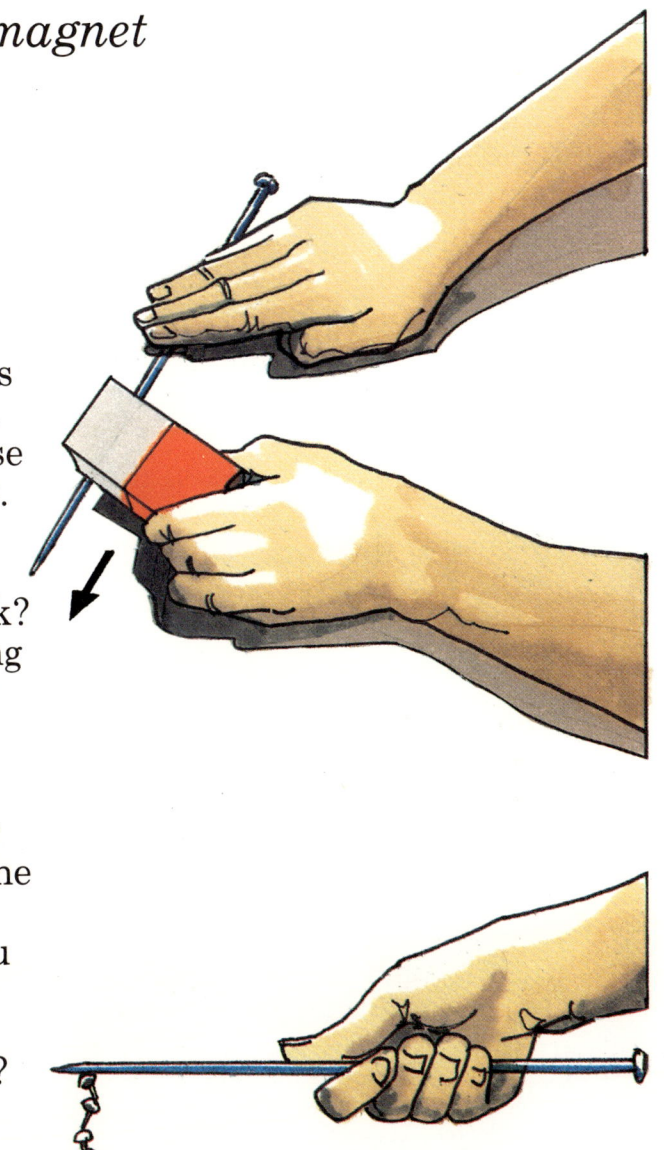

Taking care of magnets

Make a magnet from a steel knitting needle (see page 13).
How many tacks can you hang from one end of your needle magnet?
Bang your needle magnet ten times on the edge of a table.
Now how many tacks can you hang on your needle magnet?
Bang your needle magnet ten more times.
Test the strength of your needle again.
How many tacks can you hang on your needle?
What does banging a magnet do to its strength?
Always remember to treat your magnets carefully.
Avoid dropping them and always store them with a keeper.

Remagnetize your steel knitting needle.
Test the strength of your needle magnet.
Hold your needle magnet in a pair of pliers.
Ask an adult to help you heat your needle magnet.
Be careful not to burn yourself.

When your needle magnet is cool, test its strength.
What does heating a magnet do to it?

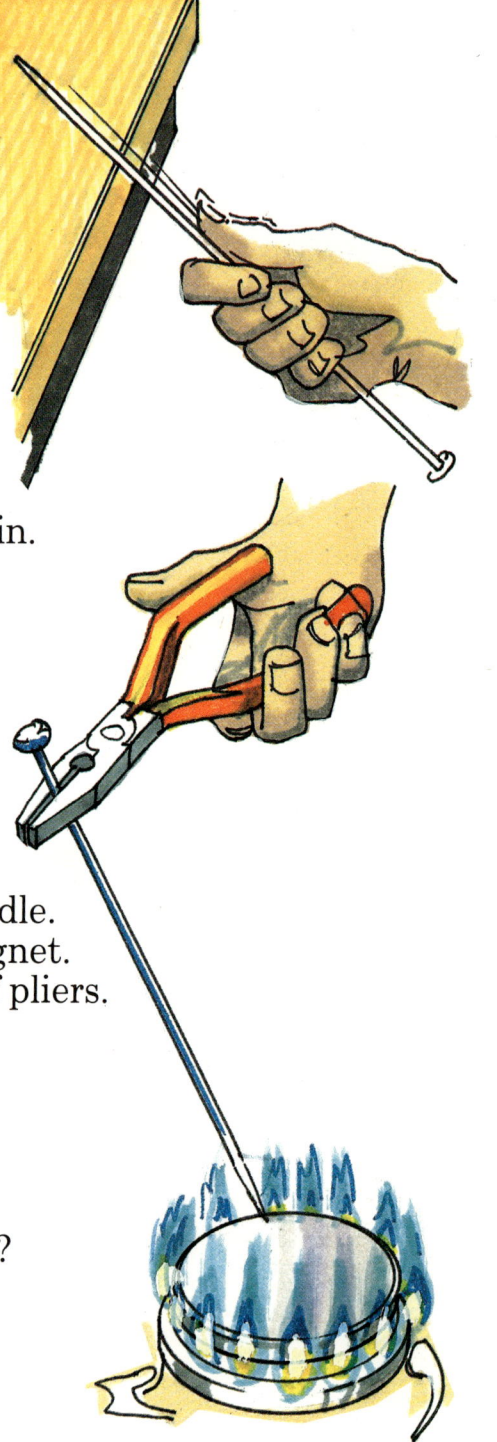

Making a magnetic compass

Make a sticky tape 'sling' to hold a bar magnet. Place the middle of your bar magnet in the sling. Press the sticky tape so that it holds the magnet.
Make a hole near each end of the sticky tape, and fix a cotton thread through the holes.

Tie a length of cotton to the middle of the cotton attached to the sling. Lift up your magnet by the cotton. Make sure the magnet can turn freely. Which way does your magnet point? Move the magnet. What happens?

If your magnet is not near anything made of iron, it will point to the magnetic north.
The end of the magnet which points north is called the north-seeking pole.

Find a cardboard or plastic carton. Cut out two opposite sides of the carton. Make a hole in the lid. Push the thread of your compass through the hole. Tape the thread in place so that the magnet hangs freely.
Let your magnet align itself.
Turn your carton so that the ends of your magnet point through the open sides.
Mark the compass directions on the top of your carton.

Making a floating compass

Stick a pin into the underside of a cork to act as a keel.
Magnetize a steel sewing needle by stroking it with a magnet (see page 13). Push the needle through the top of the cork. Float the cork in the water. Adjust the needle and the pin so that the cork floats evenly.
One drop of detergent in the water will stop the cork from moving towards the sides of the bowl.
Mark the compass points on the side of the bowl.
Christopher Columbus used a floating compass when he went to North America.

Tie a thread to the middle of a horseshoe-shaped magnet.
Make a hole in the lid of a wide-mouthed jar. Push the thread through the hole in the lid and fasten it with sticky tape. Place the lid on the jar so that the magnet hangs down and can spin freely. Mark the compass points on the lid when your magnet lines up north and south. Fill your jar with water. Will your compass work in water?
Modern compasses on ships and planes are filled with liquid to stop the indicator from swinging too much.

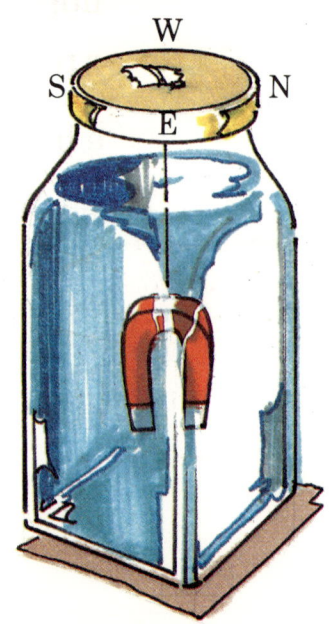

16

A magnetic compass and magnets

Hold an unmagnetized steel knitting needle close to your magnetic compass (see page 15). What happens to your compass needle?
Test both ends of your knitting needle with your compass. What happens?

Magnetize your knitting needle (see page 13).
What happens when you bring your magnetized knitting needle close to your compass needle?
Test both ends of your magnetized knitting needle. What happens?

Slowly, bring the north-seeking pole of a magnet close to the north-seeking pole of your compass needle. What happens? Do the magnetic poles attract or repel each other?

Slowly, bring the south-seeking pole of your magnet close to the north-seeking pole of your compass needle. What happens? Do the magnetic poles attract or repel each other?

What happens when you bring two south poles close together?

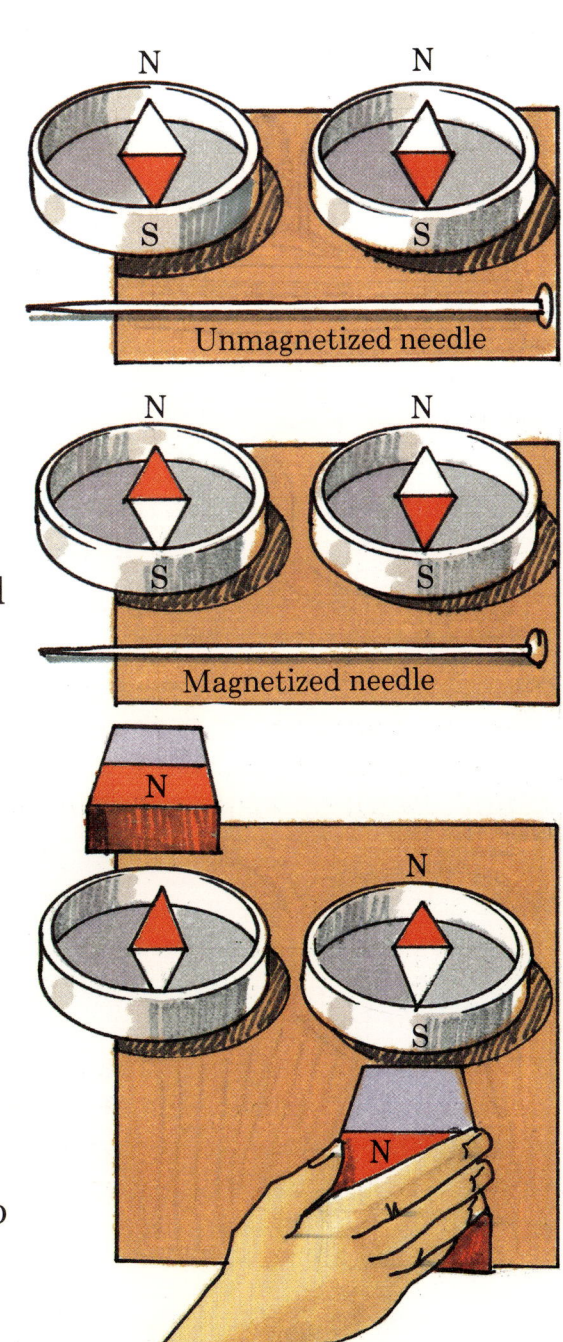

Unmagnetized needle

Magnetized needle

17

Magnetic attraction and repulsion

Find two strong bar magnets which are the same size.
Cut a block of wood the same size as your magnets.
Nail four upright sticks to the block of wood.

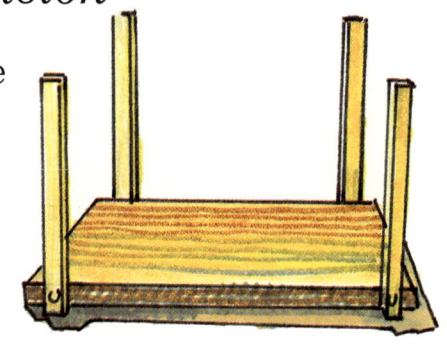

Put one bar magnet on the wooden block.
Place the other bar magnet over the first magnet. Check that the same poles are above each other.
What happens to the second magnet?
Press the second magnet down. What can you feel?

What happens if you place a third bar magnet above the second magnet with the same poles above each other?
What happens if you place your magnets with opposite poles above each other?

Make a lot of needle-and-cork floating magnetic compasses (see page 16).
Put all your floating compasses in one bowl. What happens?
Arrange your floating compasses to form different geometric patterns.
Try steering your floating compasses across the bowl using a bar magnet.

18

Comparing the strength of magnets

Put a magnetic compass on a table.
Find north, south, east and west.
Slowly, bring the north-seeking pole of a bar magnet towards your compass from the east. What happens?
Now bring the south-seeking pole towards your compass from the east. What happens?

Repeat this experiment. What happens when you bring your magnet towards the compass from the west?

Place a ruler on each side of your magnetic compass, so that one is on the east side and one is on the west side.
Place a bar magnet on each ruler.
Make sure that the south-seeking poles of your magnets are pointing towards your compass.
Make sure that your magnets are the same distance from your compass.
Is the compass needle still pointing north? If so, then your magnets are the same strength.
If not, your north-seeking compass needle points towards the stronger magnet.

Move your magnets along the rulers until the compass needle points north. You have now balanced the pull of your magnets.
How much stronger is one magnet than the other? Use this method to compare the strength of your bar magnets.

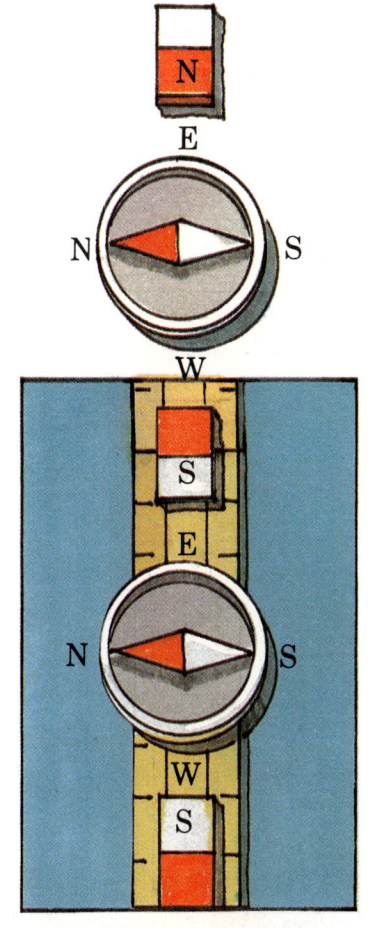

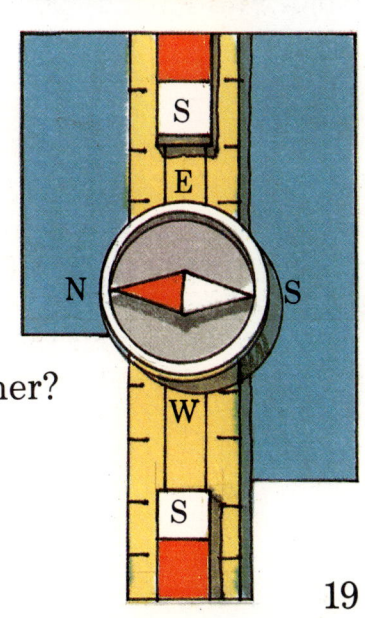

Patterns with magnets

Punch small holes in the lid of a jar. Put iron filings or cut-up pieces of steel wool into the jar and fasten the lid.

Draw a face on a sheet of cardboard. Sprinkle iron filings from your jar onto the cardboard.
Hold a magnet under the card. Move the iron filings so that your face has hair and a beard.

Place two books side by side with a bar magnet between them.
Place a thin sheet of cardboard or stiff plastic over the books and the magnet.
Sprinkle iron filings onto the card. Gently tap the card. What happens to the iron filings?
Draw the pattern your iron filings make.

Put two bar magnets side by side under the card. Make sure that the north-seeking poles are side by side. Draw the pattern that the iron filings make.

What pattern do you get if you use a horseshoe-shaped magnet?

20

Magnetic fields

Make an iron-filings pattern using only one bar magnet (see page 20).
Draw the pattern that you make.
Place a magnetic compass on the cardboard.
Which way does your compass needle point?
Move your compass on the card.
Notice how your compass needle lines up with your iron filings pattern.

Each piece of iron filing becomes a temporary magnet and lines up in the magnetic field radiating from your magnet. Your compass needle also reacts to this magnetic field.

What magnetic field pattern do you see when opposite poles of two bar magnets are attracting each other?
Draw the pattern that you see.
Is your pattern the same as the middle picture on this page?

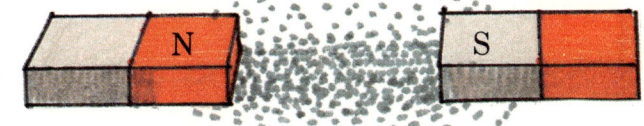

What magnetic field pattern do you see when similar poles of two bar magnets are facing each other? Draw the pattern that you see.
What patterns can you make with two magnets in other positions?
Draw the patterns you make.

Make patterns with different kinds of magnets.
What do you notice about the patterns you make?

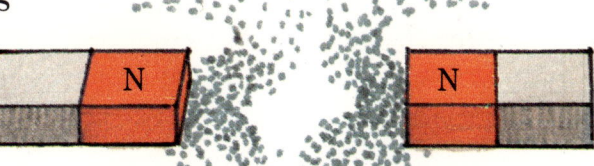

Making pictures of magnetic fields

Make an iron filings magnetic pattern (see pages 20 and 21). Use an atomizer or spray bottle to spray a fine mist of water onto your pattern. Leave your pattern undisturbed for a day. When your iron filings rust, notice how the rust stains your cardboard, giving you a picture of your pattern.

Find a sheet of waxed paper. Evenly rub the waxed paper with a candle to increase the wax layer.
Fix this waxed paper to cardboard with a paperclip, and make a magnetic pattern on the waxed paper.
Hold your cardboard with its waxed paper and pattern over a heater.
Do not bring your waxed paper near a flame, since wax catches fire easily.
The heat will soften the wax.
When the wax cools, it will hold your pattern in place.

When you record something on magnetic tape, your tape recorder makes sound patterns in the tape. Record something on tape.
Check that your recording is on the tape. Remove the tape cassette and stroke the tape with a magnet. Play your tape again. Can you hear anything?
Your magnet has altered the magnetic patterns on your recording tape.

Pencil to turn spool

Three-dimensional magnetic fields

Cut up some pieces of steel wool or use large iron filings. Sift your iron filings to remove any dust.

Put some treacle, clear honey or corn syrup into a glass jar. If you cannot get any of these, ask an adult to help you make a thick syrup from sugar and water. Stir your iron filings into the syrup, honey or treacle.

Wrap a bar magnet in a plastic bag. Tie a string to your plastic bag so that you can lower your magnet into the liquid.
Lower your magnet into the syrup mixture.
What happens? If your liquid is thick enough you should see a three-dimensional magnetic field.

Take out your magnet and replace it with an iron washer on the end of a string.
What happens when you bring a magnet to the side of the jar?

Try making other three-dimensional patterns by using one magnet inside the jar and another outside the jar.

Chapter 3   Electromagnets

Magnet power from electricity

Use a hammer and a nail to punch a hole in a length of clean steel strip from a packing case.
Push a round-headed screw through the hole and start to screw it into a block of wood.
Wind a length of bell wire around the screw before you finish screwing it into the wood. Don't forget to remove the insulation from the end of the wire.
Underneath the other side of the metal strip, screw a round-headed screw into the wood.
Wind wire around this screw.
Connect a battery to your switch using bell wire.
Place a magnetic compass on the wire.
Which way does the compass needle point?
See that the wire is in line with the compass needle.
Press down on your switch for one second.
What happens to your compass needle when electricity flows along the wire?
Switch off. What happens?
Does electricity form a magnetic field around a wire when it flows?
What happens when you connect your battery the other way around?
Remove the compass. Place a thin sheet of cardboard over the wire.
Sprinkle iron filings onto your cardboard. What happens?
Switch on. Gently tap the cardboard. What happens?

Making an electromagnet

Place your compass in a small cardboard box.
Repeat the experiment on page 24.
Does the box make any difference?

Wind your wire five times around the box.
Switch on. What happens?
Does the compass needle move more than before?
Try using a different battery.
Does the compass move more or less?
Is the second battery stronger or weaker then the first?
You have made an ammeter which will measure electricity.

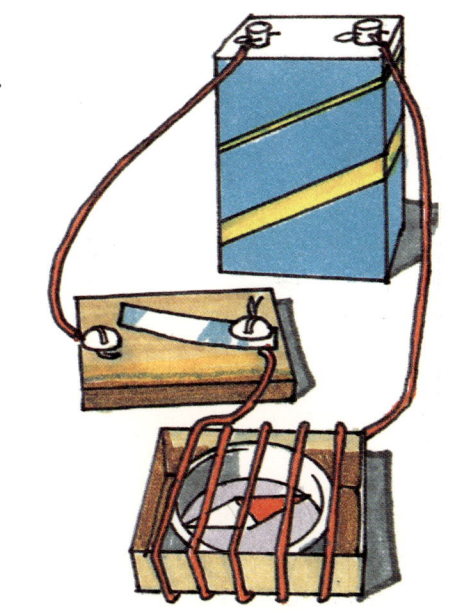

Wind your wire ten times around the box. Repeat the experiment.
Does the number of turns make any difference?

Find a large iron nail.
Test it to see if it is magnetized.
Wind a length of fine covered wire thirty times around the nail.
Make sure that you wind the wire the same way.
Connect one end of the wire to a switch and the other end to a battery.
Switch on for a second. Is your nail magnetized?
How far away will your electromagnet attract a magnetic compass?
What happens if you connect your battery the other way around?

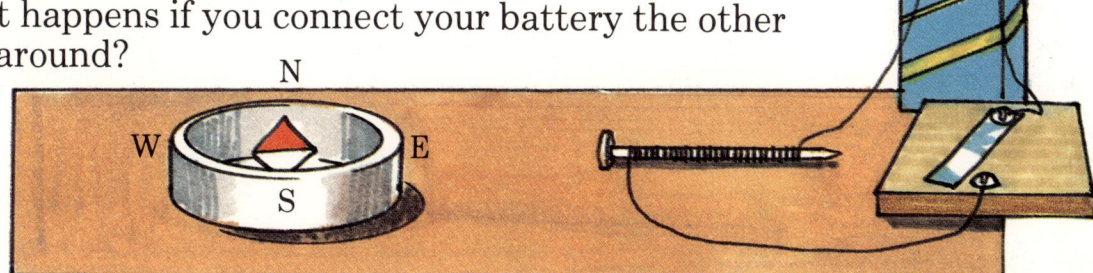

Making stronger electromagnets

Find two identical iron nails.
Test them to make sure that they are not magnetized.
Wind thirty turns of wire around one nail and fifty turns of wire around the other nail.

Connect the thirty-turn electromagnet to a battery and a switch (see page 25).
How far away does this electromagnet attract a magnetic compass needle?

Replace the thirty-turn electromagnet with the fifty-turn electromagnet.
How far away will this electromagnet attract a compass needle?
Is your fifty-turn electromagnet stronger than your thirty-turn electromagnet?
Use your electromagnets to do the experiments on pages 6, 7, 8 and 9.
Does your electromagnet act like an ordinary magnet?

Remove the nail from the coil of wire.
Does the iron nail in the coil make your electromagnet stronger or weaker?

Wind thirty-turns of wire around a wooden rod.
Is your electromagnet stronger with an iron nail or with a wooden rod?

Connect two batteries in series, with the positive terminal of one battery connected to the negative terminal of the other.
Do two batteries give you a stronger electromagnet?
Connect two batteries in parallel, positive to positive and negative to negative.
Which circuit gives the stronger electromagnet?

Making electricity from a magnet

Find a long length of covered wire. Wind ten turns of this wire around a compass in a box (see page 25).

Make a large, thirty-turn coil at the other end of the wire. Make the coil large enough for a bar magnet to pass through it.
Join the two ends of wire together to form a circuit. Make sure that the thirty-turn coil is far enough away from the compass so that your magnet does not attract the compass needle.

Slowly put the north pole of a magnet into the thirty-turn coil. What happens to the compass needle?
If the compass needle moves there must be electricity in the wire (see page 25).
Slowly withdraw the magnet.
What happens?

Slowly put the south pole of your magnet into the coil.
Which way does the compass needle move?
Which way is the electricity moving in the wire?
What happens if you put the south pole of your magnet into the coil from the other direction?

If you use a stronger magnet, will you be able to make more electricity?
How can you tell?
Do you make more electricity if you use a fifty-turn coil?
What happens if you use two magnets in your coil?
How do two magnets have to be arranged to make the most electricity?

27

Making a transformer

Make an electromagnet by winding thirty turns of covered wire around one end of a large iron nail. Connect this coil to a battery and a switch. This is called your first or primary circuit.

Find another long length of covered wire.
Wind this wire ten times around a compass in a small cardboard box. Make a coil of fifteen turns of wire at the other end. Join both ends of the wire together.
Does the compass needle move?
Is there electricity in this circuit?
This is called your second or secondary circuit.

Place the secondary coil with fifteen turns of wire onto your electromagnetic nail.
Does the compass needle move when you switch on?
Is there electricity in your secondary circuit?
As your secondary circuit is not connected to a battery, how do you think electricity forms in your secondary circuit?
What is your electromagnet doing?

If you increase the number of coils of wire in your primary circuit, the electromagnet becomes stronger. More coils of wire in your secondary circuit allow you to make more electricity. Check this by altering the number of turns in your coils. Transformers are often used in toys to 'step down' electricity to a safe voltage.

Using magnets

Electromagnets are used in telephones. When you speak into the mouthpiece, the sound pushes a diaphragm which crushes carbon granules.
This alters the conductivity of the carbon, which alters the flow of electricity in the circuit. This varying flow of electricity alters the strength of the attraction of the electromagnet and moves the diaphragm, so that your voice can be heard. The diaphragm in the earpiece is now moving in exactly the same way as the diaphragm in the mouthpiece.
Microphones and loudspeakers work in a similar way.

Electromagnets are used in tape recorders to record sounds onto magnetic tape. The sounds are played back according to the positions of the grains in the tape (see page 22).

Magnets are also used in electric motors.

How many toys do you have which use magnets?
Find out how these toys work.

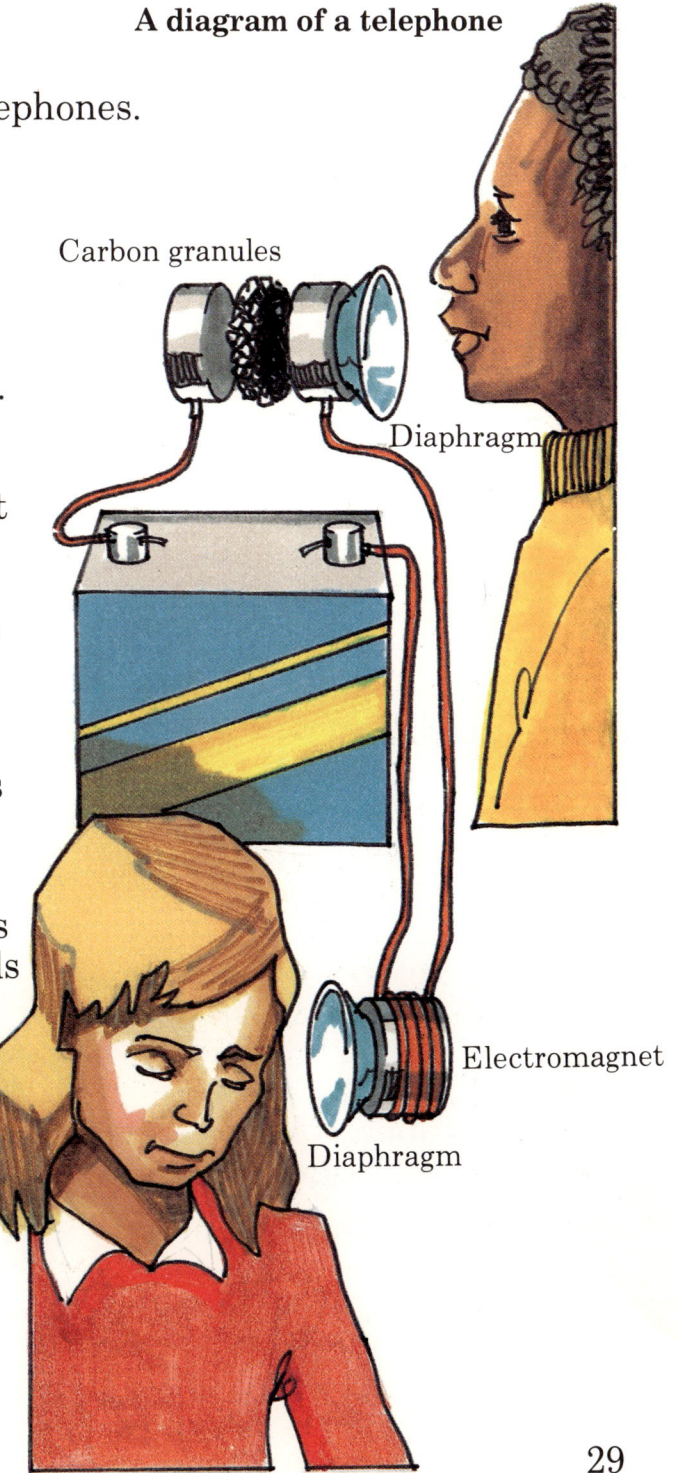

A diagram of a telephone

Carbon granules

Diaphragm

Electromagnet

Diaphragm

Chapter 4 The Earth as a magnet

Using a magnetic compass

Place your magnetic compass outside on a flat surface. Make sure that your compass is not near iron or anything that will attract the needle.
You know that your compass needle points north and south, so turn your compass until the north and south compass points are in line with the needle.
Mark the points of the compass on the ground.

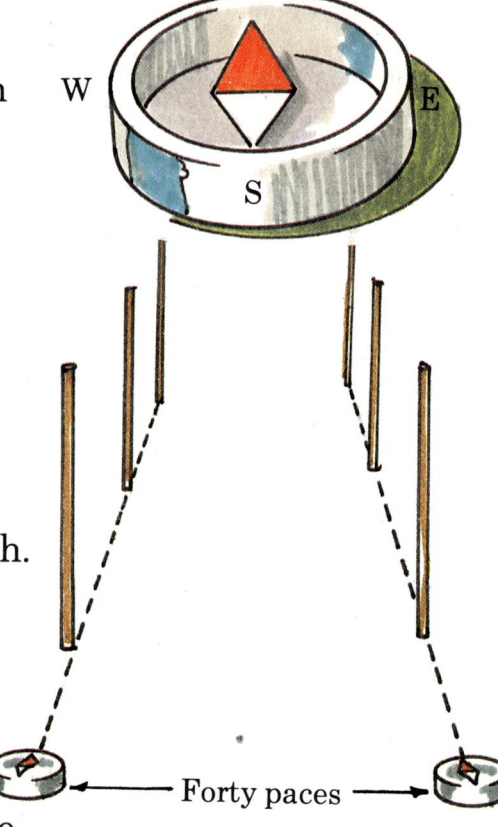

Put three sticks in the ground as far apart as you can. Make sure that the sticks are in a line pointing to magnetic north.
Walk forty paces east.
Put another three sticks in the ground in line with magnetic north.
Look at your two lines of sticks. What do you notice?
If you have placed the sticks accurately, the lines they make will meet at the north and south magnetic poles.
The sticks are also in line with the Earth's magnetic field.

Use your magnetic compass and the compass points on a map to set the map.
Have you ever used a compass as a guide when hiking?

The Earth's magnetic field

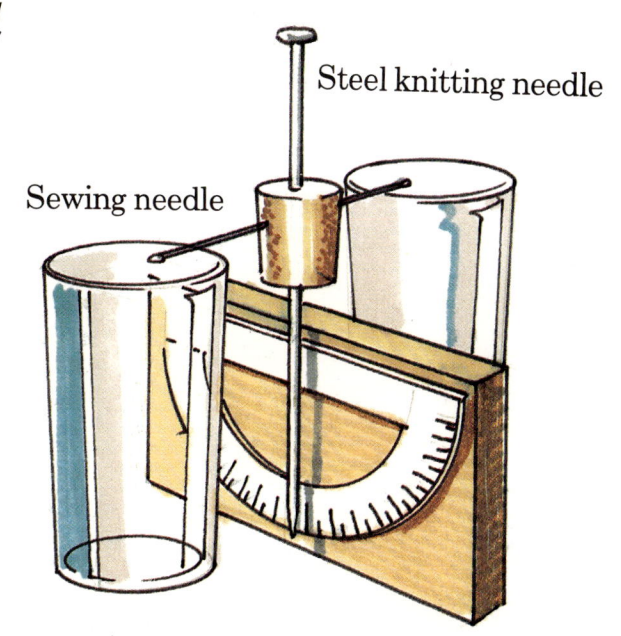

A magnetic field is in three dimensions (see page 23).
A magnetic compass measures the horizontal magnetic field.
Put a steel knitting needle through the middle of a small cork.
Stick two sewing needles into the cork from opposite sides.
Balance the cork on two glasses.
Mount a protractor on a block of wood.
See that the knitting needle points straight down to 0° on the protractor.

Magnetize the steel knitting needle with your magnet (see page 13).
In which direction does the needle point now?
Measure the angle on your protractor.
This angle of dip varies from place to place around the Earth.

Your magnetized needle will also be attracted to magnetic materials in the ground.
You can use your vertical indicator to locate iron pipes in the ground.

Locate the magnetic north pole on a map.
You will see that it is in northern Canada.
The magnetic north pole is nearly 2000 kilometres (1200 miles) from the geographic north pole.
Magnetic compasses don't point along the lines of longitude.

Making a model of the earth

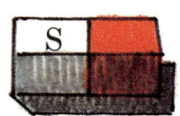

Set a magnetic compass so that the needle is in line with the north mark. Move the south pole of a bar magnet towards your compass from the east. How far is the magnet from the compass when it begins to attract the compass needle?
How far is the magnet from the compass when the needle points east? At this distance, your magnet is attracting the needle more than the Earth's magnetic pole.

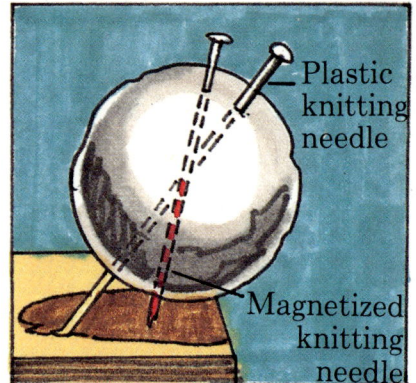

How far is the magnet from the compass when the needle points northeast?
When the needle points northeast, the force of attraction of your magnet at this distance equals the force of attraction of the Earth's magnetic north pole.
See how weak the Earth's magnetic field is near your compass, and yet it is strong enough to attract all the magnetic compasses in the world.

Look at a globe of the world. Make a large ball of modelling clay. Push a plastic knitting needle right through the middle of the ball to represent the geographical north pole.
Magnetize a steel knitting needle.
Push this needle into the clay ball to represent the north and south magnetic poles.
Use a pin to draw the shapes of the continents on your clay ball.
Make a journey around your model using a magnetic compass. Find out all you can about the Earth's magnetism.